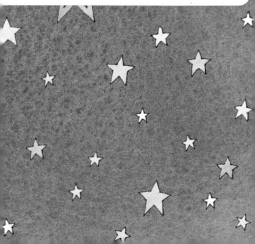

A VERY MERRY CHRISTMAS

A Very Merry Christmas

Robyn Officer

Ariel Books

**Andrews McMeel
Publishing**

Kansas City

A Very Merry Christmas

www.andrewsmcmeel.com

ISBN: 0-7407-0062-6

Library of Congress Catalog Card Number: 99-60632

A VERY MERRY CHRISTMAS

Do you start the countdown to Christmas sometime around July 25? Do you leave the tree up as long as possible? Does every room of your house, including the bathroom, have some

★ sort of decoration? If so, you truly love Christmas! Christmas is the best time of the year—a time of family get-togethers, baking tray upon tray of cookies, humming along to carols on the radio, and picking out just the right gift for everyone on your list.

There is a spirit of joy

during the Christmas season —
children eagerly await
that visit from Santa
Claus; adults can't wait
to watch the children open
presents (and to see what
St. Nick brings for them too!);
strangers go out of their
way to be kind; and we all
find ourselves with happiness
in our hearts. This delightful

book captures the wonder
that this special holiday
brings with a potpourri
of quotations, poems, carols,
and more. ♥

Merry Christmas!

I will honor
Christmas in my
heart, and try
to keep it
all the
year.

Charles Dickens
A Christmas Carol

Away in a manger,
no crib for a bed,
The little Lord Jesus
lays down his sweet head.
The stars in the sky
look down where he lay,
The little Lord Jesus
asleep in the hay.

Martin Luther

Little Jack Horner
sat in the
corner,
Eating a Christmas
pie.
He put in his
thumb, and
pulled out a

plum,
And said, "What
a good boy
am I !"

Nursery rhyme

The holly's up, the
house is all bright;
The tree is ready,
the candles alight:
Rejoice and be glad,
all children
tonight!

P. Cornelius

Jingle Bells

James Pierpont

Dashing through the snow
In a one-horse open sleigh,
O'er the fields we go
Laughing all the way;
Bells on Bobtails ring,
Making spirits bright;
What fun it is to laugh and sing
A sleighing song tonight—
Oh!

Jingle bells, jingle bells,
Jingle all the way!
Oh, what fun it is to ride
In a one-horse open sleigh!
Jingle bells, jingle bells,
Jingle all the way!
Oh, what fun it is to ride
In a one-horse open sleigh!

Early English tradition demanded that for each kiss under the mistletoe, one berry was to be removed. After all the berries were gone, the kissing would stop, and everyone involved would prosper. However, should a woman who stood under the mistletoe not be kissed, she would not be married during the coming year. ♥

SERVE THE LORD

WITH GLADNESS; COME

BEFORE HIS PRESENCE

WITH SINGING. — Psalm 100:2

I love the Christmas-
tide, and yet,
I notice this each
year I live;
I always like the
gifts I get,
But how I love the
gifts I give!

Booth Tarkington

A Christmas Recipe...

Gingerbread

Serves 6–8

8 Tbl. softened butter
3/4 cup packed brown sugar
1/4 cup molasses
2 large eggs
1 1/2 cups all-purpose flour
1 tsp. baking soda
1 Tbl. ground ginger
1/2 tsp. cinnamon
1/4 tsp. nutmeg
1/2 cup buttermilk

Preheat the oven to 350° F. Grease an 8" square pan.

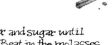

Cream the butter and sugar until light and fluffy. Beat in the molasses. Add the eggs one at a time, beating well after each one.

Sift together the flour, baking soda, and spices. Add about half of the dry ingredients to the butter mixture and beat until smooth. Add half the buttermilk and beat well. Repeat the process.

Pour the batter into the pan and bake for 30 to 40 minutes until a toothpick inserted in the center comes out clean. Cut into squares and serve warm.

Joy to the world!
The Lord is come;
Let earth receive
her King;
Let ev'ry heart
prepare Him room,
And heav'n and
nature sing...

Isaac Watts

Somehow not only
for Christmas
But all the long year
through,
The joy that you
give to others
Is the joy that comes
back to you.

And the more you
    spend in blessing
The poor and lonely
    and sad,
The more of your
    heart's possessing
Returns to make
    you glad.

John Greenleaf Whittier

CHEER

Be of
good
cheer.

William Shakespeare

The idea of the Christmas stocking began in Great Britain when Father Christmas supposedly once dropped some gold coins as he was coming down the chimney. Because someone had put their stockings out to dry over the fireplace, the coins were caught and saved. To this day, children hang their stockings on the mantelpiece in the hope that Santa will drop something inside.

JOY

is not in things,
it is in
us.

Benjamin Franklin

Silent Night

Joseph Mohr

Silent night, holy night!
    All is calm, all is bright,
'Round yon virgin Mother and Child.
    Holy infant, so tender and mild,
Sleep in heavenly peace,
    Sleep in heavenly peace.

Silent night, holy night!
    Shepherds quake at the sight.
Glories stream from heaven afar;

Heavenly hosts sing Alleluia,
Christ the Savior is born!
Christ the Savior is born.

Silent night, holy night!
Son of God, love's pure light,
Radiant beams from Thy holy face
With the dawn of redeeming grace,
Jesus, Lord, at Thy birth.
Jesus, Lord, at Thy birth.

O Christmas tree,
O Christmas
tree,
How lovely are
your branches.

German carol

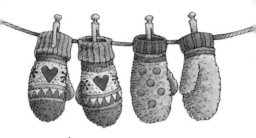

A joy that's
shared
is a joy
made double.

English proverb

At Christmas
play and
make good cheer,
for
Christmas comes
but once a
year.

Thomas Tusser

Willie, take your
little drum,
With your whistle,
Robin, come!...
When we hear the
fife and drum
Christmas should be
frolicsome.

Burgundian carol

A Christmas Recipe...

ANGEL FOOD CAKE

Serves 8-10

12 large egg whites, room temperature
1 tsp. cream of tartar
1¼ cups sugar
1 tsp. vanilla extract
1 cup sifted cake flour

Preheat the oven to 375°F.

Beat the egg whites and cream of tartar at high speed until foamy. With the

mixer still at high speed, beat in the
sugar a little at a time, until the whites
form stiff peaks. Gently fold in the
vanilla.

Sprinkle a third of the flour over the
egg whites and gently fold in. Repeat
twice.

Scrape the batter into an ungreased
9" tube pan and bake for about 40 minutes until the cake is springy. Turn
the pan upside down over the neck
of a bottle or funnel and let the cake
cool completely before removing
it from the pan. Serve with fresh
fruit.

MERRY

Yes, Virginia, there
is a Santa Claus.
He exists as certainly
as love and generosity
and devotion exist.

Francis P. Church

On the first
day of Christmas,
My true love
sent to me
A partridge in
a pear tree.

hree French hens... Four calling birds...

Five golden rings... Six geese a-laying...

Traditional

Seven Swans a-swimming... Eight maids a

Heap on more wood! –
the wind is chill;
But let it whistle
as it will,
We'll keep our
Christmas
merry still.

Sir Walter Scott

O holy night,
the stars are
brightly shining;
It is the night
of the dear
Savior's birth.

John Sullivan Dwight

Saint Nicholas, originally a bishop in Asia Minor, became the patron saint of Russia. During the Middle Ages, presents were given on his feast day, which was December 6. In time, Saint Nicholas came to be associated with a number of miracles about children and gift-giving.

I'm dreaming of a white Christmas.

Irving Berlin

CHEER

If you have much,
give of your wealth;
if you have little,
give of your heart.

Arab proverb

A Christmas Recipe...

EGGNOG

Serves 10

8 eggs, separated
6 Tbl. sugar
6 cups milk
Rum or rum flavoring to taste
2 cups heavy cream
Nutmeg

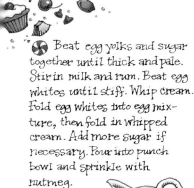 Beat egg yolks and sugar together until thick and pale. Stir in milk and rum. Beat egg whites until stiff. Whip cream. Fold egg whites into egg mixture, then fold in whipped cream. Add more sugar if necessary. Pour into punch bowl and sprinkle with nutmeg.

And the angel
said unto them,
Fear not: for, behold,
I bring you
good tidings
of great joy,
which shall be to
all people.

Luke 2:10

Christmas Is Coming

OldEnglish carol

Christmas is coming, the
geese are getting fat,

Please to put a penny in
the old man's hat;

If you haven't got a penny,
a ha'penny will do,

If you haven't got a
ha'penny, God bless
you.

The stockings
were hung
by the chimney
with care,
In hopes that
St. Nicholas
soon would be
there.

Clement Clarke Moore

Holly, with its prickly leaves, represents the crown of thorns that Jesus wore.

The first decorated Christmas tree appeared in Strasbourg, Germany, in 1605. Other countries adopted the idea, and before long Christmas trees were common throughout Scandinavia, Russia, and Europe.

JOY
is the feeling of
GRINNING
inside.

Dr. Melba Colgrove

*Not what
we give,
but what we
share,
for the gift
without the giver
is bare.*

James Russell Lowell

A Christmas Recipe...

CRANBERRY BREAD

Serves 8-10

6 Tbl. softened butter
2/3 cup sugar
2 large eggs
2 cups all-purpose flour
1 tsp. baking powder
1/2 tsp. baking soda
1/4 tsp. salt
1 cup chopped cranberries
1/4 cup buttermilk
1/2 cup chopped pecans

Preheat the oven to 350°F. Grease a 9"x5" loaf pan.

Cream the butter and sugar until light and fluffy. Add the eggs one at a time, beating well after each one.

Sift together the flour, baking powder, baking soda, and salt. Mix the cranberries and buttermilk. Alternate beating the flour and cranberry mixtures into the butter mixture, beginning and ending with the flour. Stir in the nuts.

Spread the batter in the pan and bake for about 50 minutes until a toothpick inserted in the center comes out clean. Let cool in the pan for about 5 minutes and then turn the bread onto a wire rack to cool.

What can I give Him,
    Poor as I am?
If I were a shepherd
    I would bring a lamb,
If I were a wise man
    I would do my part,
Yet what can I give Him?
Give Him my heart.

Christina Rosetti

It Came upon a
Midnight
Clear

Edmund H. Sears

It came upon a midnight clear,
That glorious song of old,
From angels bending near the earth,
To touch their harps of gold!
"Peace on the earth, good will to men,
From heaven's all gracious King!"
The world in solemn stillness lay
To hear the angels sing.

Still through the cloven skies
they come
With peaceful wings unfurled
And still their heavenly music floats
O'er all the weary world;
Above its sad and lowly plains
They bend on hovering wing.
And ever o'er its Babel sounds
The blessed angels sing.

Now thrice
welcome, Christmas.
Which brings us
good cheer,
Minc'd pies and
plum-porridge,
Good ale and strong
beer;

With pig, goose,
and capon.
The best that may be,
So well doth the
weather
And our stomachs
agree.

Christmas song

CHEER

A glad
heart
makes a
cheerful
countenance...

Proverbs 15:13

"God bless us every one!" said Tiny Tim, the last of all.

Charles Dickens